Look Out, Butterfly!

Devised and photographed
by Nic Bishop

Collins

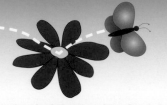

A storymap

Ideas for guided reading

Learning objectives: track the text in the correct order; recount the main points in sequence; use terms about books: book, cover, beginning, end, page, title; ask questions about why things happen.

Curriculum links: Mathematical development: Use everyday words to describe position; Knowledge and understanding of the world: Find out about and identify features of living things

Interest words: butterfly

Resources: Paint and paper

Getting started

- Ask the children to look carefully at the front cover and predict the title. Discuss the terms 'book cover' and 'title'. *What is the book about?*

- Discuss what kind of book this is (non-fiction). Ask why there are photos (it is a book about something that really happened).

- Walk through the book up to p11 with the children and ask what is happening. *What is the butterfly doing? What colour flowers does it visit?* Can the children predict what will happen next? Have they noticed the crab spider in the flower?

- Model how to use words like 'beginning', 'then', 'after that', 'in the end' to retell the events in the correct sequence.

- Ask the children to look through the book and point out the title, the front cover, the beginning and the end.

Reading and responding

- Ask the children to 'read' the book together to p13, saying what happens. Prompt and praise correct left to right movement and page turning. Praise the use of position words like 'on', 'in', 'up', and use of colour words to describe the flowers.

- Discuss what the crab spider wants to do and why the butterfly didn't notice the crab spider. Did they guess the ending?